D1483277

J B DRAKE 2009
Nick, Charles,1960-
Sir Francis Drake :
slave trader and pirate /

033109

WITHDRAWN

When the Queen did knight Drake,
she did then knight the arrantest knave,
the vilest villain, the falsest thief,
and the cruelest murderer that ever was born.

John Doughty, brother of a ship captain
Drake had executed for mutiny in 1578

This book is dedicated to my own beloved buccaneers, Julian and Azize.

Photographs © 2009: akg-Images, London/Theodor de Bry: 90; Art Resource, NY: 51 (Frank Moss Bennett/Private Collection), 10 (British Library, London/HIP), 26 (Theodor de Bry/Bildarchiv Preussischer Kulturbesitz), 57 (John Goldar/The New York Public Library), 37, 78 center (Erich Lessing), 77 bottom, 39 (The New York Public Library), 74 top (The Stapleton Collection); Bridgeman Art Library International Ltd., London/New York: 19 (Hendrick Danckerts/Yale Center for British Art, Paul Mellon Collection, USA), 78 top (Howard Davie/Private Collection), 76 bottom (Fernao Vaz Dourado/Arquivo Nacional da Torre do Tombo, Lisbon, Portgual/Giraudon), 84 (Sir John Gilbert/ Private Collection/Ken Welsh), 36, 75 bottom (George Gower/Private Collection/Philip Mould Ltd, London), 100 (Daniel Mytens/His Grace The Duke of Norfolk, Arundel Castle), 60 (Private Collection), 79 center (Private Collection/Ken Welsh), 104, 105 (Private Collection/Rafael Valls Gallery, London, UK), 73 (Paul Rainer/Private Collection/Look and Learn); Corbis Images: 32, 66, 67, 70, 117 (Bettmann), 74 center (Stapleton Collection); Getty Images: 34, 75 top, 79 bottom, 119 (Hulton Archive), 74 bottom (Popperfoto); Mary Evans Picture Library: 44, 52, 79 top, 96 (Douglas McCarthy), 46; National Geographic Image Collection/ Jean-Leon Huens: 76 top, 77 top; The Art Archive/Picture Desk: 21, 78 bottom; The Granger Collection, New York: 22 (Theodor de Bry), 76 center, 91.

Illustrations by XNR Productions, Inc.: 4, 5, 8, 9
Cover art, page 8 inset by Mark Summers
Chapter art by Raphael Montoliu

Library of Congress Cataloging-in-Publication Data
Nick, Charles, 1960-
Sir Francis Drake : slave trader and pirate / Charles Nick.
p. cm. — (A wicked history)
Includes bibliographical references and index.
ISBN-13: 978-0-531-21800-6 (lib. bdg.) 978-0-531-20740-6 (pbk.)
ISBN-10: 0-531-21800-7 (lib. bdg.) 0-531-20740-4 (pbk.)
1. Drake, Francis, Sir, 1540?-1596—Juvenile literature. 2. Great Britain—History, Naval—Tudors, 1485-1603—Biography—Juvenile literature. 3. Great Britain—History—Elizabeth, 1558-1603—Biography—Juvenile literature. 4. Explorers—Great Britain—Biography—Juvenile literature. 5. Admirals—Great Britain—Biography—Juvenile literature. 6. Privateering—History—16th century—Juvenile literature. I. Title.
DA86.22.D7N53 2009
942.05'5092dc22
[B]
2008041605

Tod Olson, Series Editor
Marie O'Neill, Art Director
Allicette Torres, Cover Design
SimonSays Design!, Book Design and Production

© 2009 Scholastic Inc.

1 2 3 4 5 6 7 8 9 10 R 18 17 16 15 14 13 12 11 10 09   23

Sir Francis Drake

Slave Trader and Pirate

CHARLES NICK

Franklin Watts®
An Imprint of Scholastic Inc.
New York Toronto London Auckland Sydney
Mexico City New Delhi Hong Kong
Danbury, Connecticut

The World of Sir Francis Drake

For three decades, Drake chased Spanish ships around the globe,
battling for gold, silver, and control of the seas.

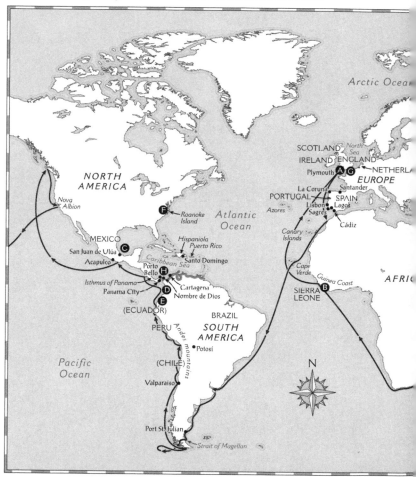

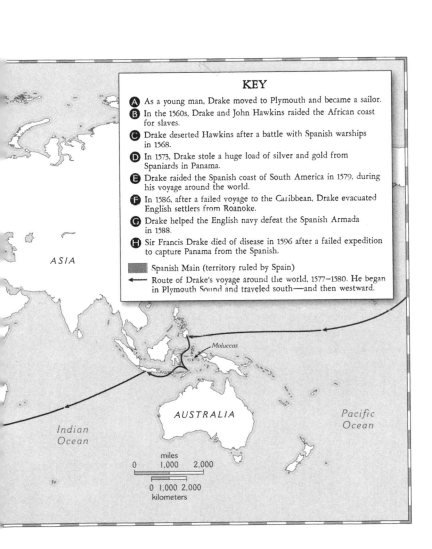

KEY

A As a young man, Drake moved to Plymouth and became a sailor.

B In the 1560s, Drake and John Hawkins raided the African coast for slaves.

C Drake deserted Hawkins after a battle with Spanish warships in 1568.

D In 1573, Drake stole a huge load of silver and gold from Spaniards in Panama.

E Drake raided the Spanish coast of South America in 1579, during his voyage around the world.

F In 1586, after a failed voyage to the Caribbean, Drake evacuated English settlers from Roanoke.

G Drake helped the English navy defeat the Spanish Armada in 1588.

H Sir Francis Drake died of disease in 1596 after a failed expedition to capture Panama from the Spanish.

Spanish Main (territory ruled by Spain)

⬅ Route of Drake's voyage around the world, 1577–1580. He began in Plymouth Sound and traveled south—and then westward.

ASIA

Moluccas

AUSTRALIA

Indian Ocean

Pacific Ocean

miles
0   1,000   2,000

0 1,000 2,000
kilometers

TABLE OF CONTENTS

A Wicked Web

A look at the allies and enemies of Sir Francis Drake.

Family and Friends

WILLIAM HAWKINS
businessman in Plymouth;
also a pirate

JOHN HAWKINS
William's son;
slave trader and pirate

EDMUND DRAKE
Drake's father

**THOMAS, JOHN, JOSEPH,
AND EDWARD DRAKE**
Drake's brothers

SIR FRANCIS DRAKE

MARY NEWMAN
Drake's first wife

ELIZABETH SYDENHAM
Drake's second wife

Kings and Queens

∾∾∾∾∾∾∾∾∾∾∾∾∾∾∾∾∾∾∾∾

QUEEN ELIZABETH I
English monarch and sponsor
of Drake's expeditions

KING PHILIP II
Spanish king and sworn
enemy of England

Mutineers and Mariners

∾∾∾∾∾∾∾∾∾∾∾∾∾∾∾∾∾∾∾∾∾

THOMAS DOUGHTY
sea captain executed by
Drake for alleged mutiny

JOHN DOUGHTY
brother of Thomas; accused
of plotting to kill Drake

FRANCIS FLETCHER
minister persecuted by Drake

WILLIAM BOROUGH
sea captain accused
by Drake of mutiny

NUNO DE SILVA
mariner who helped Drake
navigate the coast of
South America

LORD CHARLES HOWARD
Drake's commander
during the battle with
the Spanish Armada

DUKE OF MEDINA-SIDONIA
admiral of the Spanish Armada

SIR FRANCIS DRAKE, c. 1540–1596

Santo Domingo, Hispaniola, January 1586

THE SIGHT OF ONE PIRATE SHIP WOULD have been frightening enough. But when residents of Santo Domingo looked out to sea one morning early in January 1586, they saw *dozens* of pirate ships. Then came word that the men in those vessels had landed nearby and were preparing to attack.

Santo Domingo was a large and fairly well-defended city. It had been the first Spanish settlement in the Caribbean and still shone as a jewel of Spain's empire in the Americas. But on this day its residents had good reason to be scared.

The commander of the pirate fleet had made himself known and feared in all the far-flung lands of the Spanish Empire. He had ransacked Spanish ships and settlements from the Atlantic coast of Africa to the Pacific coast of South America. He had plundered many fortunes in Spanish silver and gold. He had sent dozens of Spanish ships to the bottom of the sea. Now he was leading hundreds of well-armed invaders toward Santo Domingo.

Some residents grabbed guns and went forward to fight the Englishmen. But when they saw what they were up against, "many shamelessly abandoned their arms," one resident later recalled. They ran away to hide in the countryside, allowing Drake's pirates to enter Santo Domingo as easily "as a man enters his own house," another Spaniard described.

The people of Santo Domingo watched in horror as the English set fire to their town, burning down more than half its buildings. When their work was done, the pirates demanded loot from the city's leaders. They collected 25,000 gold coins and then left the city in ruins. "The evils which have befallen us . . . cannot be recounted without tears," wrote one resident. Added another: "Nothing remains but life itself."

With his newfound treasure in hand, the English commander climbed aboard one of his ships and sailed away. He would not soon be forgotten. His name was Sir Francis Drake.

When Drake returned to England, he would be greeted the way he had come to expect—as a hero. Drake's exploits at sea had made him rich and famous. He had sailed around the globe—only the second person in history to accomplish the feat. He had terrorized Spain, England's rival for control of the world's oceans. His swashbuckling raids had added gold to England's treasury and disrupted Spanish trade routes at sea. For service to his country, the queen had made him a knight, one of England's highest honors.

To his countrymen, Drake was a brilliant mariner and a daring military leader. To the Spanish, he was little more than a criminal.

More than 400 years later, Sir Francis Drake is still a legend. But who was this famous sailor? A great explorer—or a gold-hungry, lawless pirate?

PART 1

Education of a Pirate

CHAPTER 1

Schooled at Sea

A country boy
LEARNS TO SAIL AND
TO STEAL.

IMAGINE YOURSELF ON A BEACH STARING out into a thick gray fog. You can't tell the ships from the shadows. Nothing is clear.

That's what it's like to try to make sense of Francis Drake's early years. So little is known about his childhood that even the exact year of his birth is a mystery. Historians know only that he was born between 1538 and 1543. No one even knows his mother's name.

Francis's father was a man named Edmund Drake. It's not exactly clear what kind of man he was. Some people described him as a preacher who devoted himself to God. But he may have been little more than a common criminal. In 1548, someone named Edmund Drake took part in several robberies near Tavistock, England, where Francis grew up. On one occasion, this Edmund Drake teamed up with some companions and stole a horse. Another time, he beat up a man and ran off with his money.

Was Drake's father a preacher or a robber? Good or wicked? It's possible, of course, that he had both qualities in ample supply. If so, young Francis turned out to be much like his father.

Francis Drake spent much of his childhood in Devon, a county in southwestern England that juts out into the Atlantic Ocean. He grew up in farming country near Tavistock, but by the time he was a teenager, he had moved to the port of Plymouth to live with wealthy relatives. Plymouth was only about 15 miles from where he was born. But for a country boy like Drake, it must have seemed like an entirely different world.

Plymouth bustled with all the activity of a busy port city. Huge ships sailed into the harbor every day carrying food, spices, merchandise, and people from all over the world.

When the teenaged Drake arrived in Plymouth, sailors were in great demand. The Spanish and Portuguese had been exploring the globe for half a century. They had settlements in Africa, Asia, and South America. They boasted the best ships, the most talented mapmakers, and the most experienced sea captains in the world. But the English queen, Elizabeth I, wanted to challenge Spain and Portugal for control of the high seas. For the sea captains and sailors of Plymouth, this meant a chance to explore the world—and to come home rich.

The most successful of these English adventurers were Drake's own relatives—the ruthless members of the Hawkins family. The head of the family, William

WHEN FRANCIS DRAKE was a teenager, he moved to the
bustling port city of Plymouth, where his relative William
Hawkins operated a large fleet of merchant ships.

Hawkins, was about 50 years older than young Francis
Drake. He had built one of the largest fortunes in
Plymouth by trading merchandise in distant lands.
His ships carried cloth, tin, and other English goods to
sell at ports on the European continent. They brought
back salt, wine, sugar, pepper, soap, and fish to sell in
England.

In the early 1530s, William Hawkins expanded his
business. He became the first Englishman to regularly

send vessels across the Atlantic Ocean to South America. His ship captains brought back brazilwood, a highly prized wood used to dye clothes red. On the way to South America, Hawkins's ships stopped in Africa. There, his captains bargained for the tusks of slaughtered elephants. This gleaming white ivory sold for a fortune to wealthy Europeans.

Each journey added to the wealth and reputation of William Hawkins. The people of Plymouth considered him a well-respected member of the community. They even elected him mayor for a time.

But Hawkins also had a dark side. In addition to trading with other merchants, his sea captains attacked and robbed ships from foreign countries. William Hawkins, businessman, was also a pirate.

One of his sons, John Hawkins, seemed eager to follow in his father's footsteps. John was about ten years older than Francis Drake. He had an ambitious streak and a taste for violence. At the age of 20—around the time that Drake arrived in Plymouth—John got into a fight and killed a man. His powerful father managed to get him a pardon from the queen.

John Hawkins was smart, brave, and sometimes just plain cruel. That made him the perfect person to teach Francis Drake the art of piracy.

From an early age, Drake sailed regularly on ships that were owned and sometimes commanded by John Hawkins. During these adventures, Drake learned how to navigate the oceans. He also learned how to chase other ships at sea, attack them, and seize their treasure. By the time he was 20, Drake was already an experienced pirate.

DRAKE'S COUSIN JOHN HAWKINS was a brave and skilled mariner. He was also a murderous pirate who taught Drake the art of looting foreign merchant ships.

WEALTH OF THE NEW WORLD

WHEN FRANCIS DRAKE WAS JUST A BOY, THE Spanish were busy extending their control over Central and South America. They had conquered vast civilizations from Mexico to Peru and plundered tons of gold and silver. Now, high in the rugged Andes mountains, they discovered a treasure bigger than any yet found—the silver mines of Potosí.

The rich Potosí mine, when added to the other conquests of the Spanish Empire, gave Spain an almost endless source of wealth. From the early 1500s to the mid 1600s, Spanish ships sailed home with more than 35 million pounds of silver from American mines—enough to triple the existing amount in all of Europe.

MANY THOUSANDS of Indians died while being forced to mine silver for the Spanish.

SPAIN AND PORTUGAL DOMINATE

The English were desperate to get a share of these dazzling riches. But so far, their overseas empire lagged far behind the two big world powers, Spain and Portugal. In 1494, just two years after Christopher Columbus landed in America, the Spanish and Portuguese had signed a treaty splitting all the lands of the New World between themselves.

Then in 1497, the English sent their first explorer to the New World. John Cabot explored the coastline of what is now Canada and claimed its lands for England.

English adventurers began to dream of setting up colonies in the New World, where they hoped to find silver and gold of their own.

Francis Drake and John Hawkins had their own scheme for getting their hands on the wealth of the New World—stealing it. After all, they figured, the Spanish had grabbed the loot without any concern for England. So why shouldn't they, as Englishmen, just grab it back?

CHAPTER 2

Trafficking in Humans

The young mariner becomes involved in an EVIL ENTERPRISE.

By THE TIME FRANCIS DRAKE REACHED his twenties, he was an experienced sailor. With Hawkins in command, he may well have taken part in raids on merchant ships. But those expeditions were of little consequence compared to the raid the two pirates were about to launch—a raid that would haunt the world for centuries.

In 1562, Drake probably took part in an expedition that opened one of the most brutally destructive trading routes in the history of the world. In October of that year, John Hawkins sailed from Plymouth with a fleet of four ships and a crew of 100 men—apparently including the young Drake. They headed for the west coast of Africa, where they planned to kidnap hundreds of Africans and sell them as slaves.

When Hawkins set out on his expedition, the Portuguese had already been trading in slaves for more than half a century. In the late 1400s, Portuguese slave traders began settling along the west coast of Africa, where they traded European goods and guns for kidnapped Africans. Portuguese ships carried many of these captives to the New World and sold them to settlers in Spanish or Portuguese colonies.

John Hawkins sailed from Plymouth determined to get his own piece of the transatlantic slave trade. Even before he reached the coast of Africa, his pirates captured a half-dozen Portuguese ships. They seized

GROWING SUGAR WAS PROFITABLE for Spanish landowners in Hispaniola. But it was deadly for the enslaved Africans they forced to work their fields. Drake took part in raids to kidnap Africans and sell them into slavery in the New World.

valuable cargoes of cloves, wax, and ivory, as well as enslaved Africans. They continued down the Guinea Coast of Africa to Sierra Leone, about 4,000 miles south of England. In the end, they rounded up between 300 and 400 captives—"partly by the sword and partly by other means," according to one contemporary account. Hawkins then sent a small ship back to England, carrying some of the plundered merchandise. Francis Drake was apparently aboard that vessel.

The other ships, meanwhile, set sail for the New World on a journey that proved indescribably horrible for the Africans onboard. Hawkins crowded them into dark and stuffy spaces below deck, where they had to survive on small rations of beans and water. As many as half of the captives died during the journey.

Hawkins took the Africans to the Spanish island of Hispaniola in the Caribbean Sea. Spain had banned Englishmen from doing business in the New World. But many Spanish colonists were willing to ignore the ban—especially since Hawkins was selling the Africans at low prices. He returned to England in September 1563 with a fortune in gold, silver, pearls, sugar, ginger, and animal hides—most of it collected in payment for the African slaves.

Hawkins's first slave-trading expedition was so successful that he soon made plans for a second one. Queen Elizabeth warned that if any Africans were "carried away without their free consent, it would be detestable." She also said that Englishmen who bought or sold other human beings could expect "the vengeance of Heaven" as punishment. But Elizabeth knew that slave trading could bring huge profits—and the money would make her kingdom stronger. In the end, she failed to back up her public objections to the slave trade. In fact, she loaned Hawkins a ship from the Royal Navy to help him transport his captives.

Hawkins, with help from his queen and Francis Drake, had launched one of the worst horrors in human history. By the 1700s, the English dominated the transatlantic slave trade. When the slave trade finally came to an end in 1870, about ten million Africans had been put in chains and taken to the Americas against their will.

In all, Hawkins led three slave-trading expeditions to the New World in the 1560s. Drake may have been involved in all of them. We know for sure that he played an important role in the final one. On that trip, he wasn't just a common sailor. For the first time, he commanded his own ship—and the decisions he made would haunt him for the rest of his life.

CHAPTER 3

A Coward?

With lives on the line, Francis Drake
DISAPPEARS INTO THE NIGHT.

A FLEET OF SIX SHIPS SAILED OUT OF
Plymouth Sound in October 1567. John Hawkins
commanded a huge vessel called the *Jesus of Lubeck*,
owned by Queen Elizabeth. At some point in the
journey, Francis Drake took command of a smaller
ship, the *Judith*.

The voyage went badly from the start. Four days
into the trip, a howling storm scattered the fleet. The
ships eventually managed to regroup, but more trouble
awaited them on the African coast.

At Cape Verde, the westernmost part of Africa, Hawkins organized a raiding party to capture Africans and went ashore. Local villagers fought off the Englishmen with a barrage of poisoned arrows. Hawkins and 25 of his party were wounded. Seven or eight of the pirates eventually died.

The expedition ran into more trouble farther south, on the Guinea Coast. Hawkins had no luck finding captives, so he allied himself with two local chiefs who wanted help fighting a neighboring tribe. Drake took part in these battles, which led to the deaths of about 60 Englishmen and the capture of several hundred Africans.

Hawkins and Drake then set sail for the New World, their human cargo chained in the holds of their ships. More than 100 of the captives may have died during the dismal journey to the New World.

When Hawkins and Drake arrived in the Caribbean, selling the Africans proved to be as treacherous as capturing them. Hawkins hoped to sell his captives

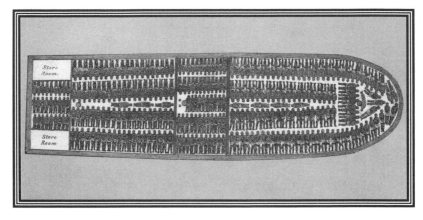

THIS DIAGRAM SHOWS how kidnapped Africans were crowded onto English slave ships. Conditions on the ships were so horrible that slave traders like Drake could expect about one of every five captives to die during an ocean crossing.

on the Caribbean coast of South America—a region known as the Spanish Main. But most Spanish colonists there refused to do business with the Englishmen. Settlers in one town fired cannons at Hawkins's ships. In another, Hawkins became so frustrated that he sent 200 armed men ashore. They burned down buildings, stole money, and kidnapped local residents. Hawkins refused to release the hostages until the people of the town bought some of the Africans he had captured.

Finally, in August 1568, the English ships headed for home. Just days into the journey, they ran into a fierce storm. Howling winds and huge waves swept over the fleet, leaving many of the vessels badly damaged. Hawkins realized that they wouldn't survive the ocean crossing without first making repairs. So he guided his ships to San Juan de Ulúa, a Spanish port in Mexico. An even worse disaster awaited them there.

At first, local officials agreed to let Hawkins and Drake anchor their damaged ships near a little island offshore. But on the morning of September 23, 1568, the Spanish mounted a surprise attack. "Fear nothing!" Hawkins shouted. But cannonballs rained down on the English fleet, shredding the sails and masts of the biggest pirate ship, the *Jesus of Lubeck*. The vessel was so badly damaged that Hawkins and his men had to abandon it. Some of the men, including Hawkins, climbed into a vessel called the *Minion*. Others clambered aboard Francis Drake's little ship, the *Judith*.

Drake and Hawkins led their ships away from the

HAWKINS AND DRAKE'S SHIPS (right) exchange cannon fire with Spanish warships. After the fighting, Drake slipped back to England, abandoning 100 countrymen to face certain death or enslavement.

battle. That night, they anchored along the Mexican coast and took stock of the damage. No other ship had survived. And when the sun came up the next morning, Hawkins received more bad news. The *Judith* was gone. Francis Drake had sneaked off and sailed for home.

Drake's desertion left Hawkins in grave danger. The *Minion* was badly damaged and overcrowded. With so many people aboard, food and fresh water would run out long before they made it back to England. In the end, Hawkins had to leave about 100 of his men behind in Mexico. Some starved in the forests or were killed by Native Americans. Others fell into the hands of the Spanish, who murdered, imprisoned, or enslaved them.

Drake and Hawkins both made it back to England alive. But 200 to 300 of their companions never returned. Hawkins was furious with Drake for abandoning his fellow Englishmen. The young pirate, Hawkins said, "forsook us in our great misery."

But was Drake really a coward and a deserter? Or was he simply a good officer trying to save his own men in a life-or-death situation? Those questions would follow him for the rest of his life.

The journey left Francis Drake with a burning desire to prove himself. This time, the Spanish had humiliated him. The next time, he would get his revenge.

RELIGIOUS RIVALS

WHEN DRAKE RETURNED FROM HIS DISASTROUS voyage to the New World, tensions between England and Spain were on the rise, thanks in part to a religious revolution that was splitting Europe in two.

The revolt began in a German state, with Martin Luther, a disillusioned priest. Luther broke with the Catholic Church, which had controlled religious life in Europe for centuries. Luther and his followers soon became known

as Protestants, and the movement to break from the Catholic Church became known as the Protestant Reformation.

Francis Drake was a passionate Protestant.

QUEEN ELIZABETH I outlawed Catholicism and made England Protestant.

Even as a young sailor, he tried to convert his shipmates to the new faith. He must have been overjoyed when Queen Elizabeth I outlawed Catholic worship in England in 1559. Now England was a Protestant country.

Spain, on the other hand, remained fiercely Catholic. Under the reign of King Philip II, Protestants were harshly punished. People who rejected Catholic teachings could be burned to death for their beliefs. According to one story, Philip vowed that he "would bring the wood to burn my own son" if the child became a Protestant. Philip began plotting to overthrow Elizabeth and return her nation to Catholicism.

PHILIP II OF SPAIN
fought to make all of
Europe Catholic.

CHAPTER 4

On His Own

Drake brings home one treasure—AND DREAMS OF A BIGGER PRIZE.

In July 1569, Francis Drake married a woman named Mary Newman. The couple spent all of four months together before Drake grew restless. Nearing 30 years old, he was eager to earn his reputation as a great mariner and a relentless foe of Spain.

Not long after he got married, Drake found merchants to fund a new set of raids so that he could return to sea. His plan was to get rich and take revenge on the Spanish at the same time.

IN 1571, DRAKE SAILED back to the Caribbean in search of
more plunder. He and his men looted Spanish ships, killed
Spanish sailors, and stripped a Catholic friar naked. Still, Drake
dreamed of a more daring adventure ahead.

By February 1571, Drake was in the Caribbean again,
in command of a small vessel called the *Swan*. Near the
Spanish colony of Panama, Drake and his men joined
forces with some French pirates. Prowling the coast and

a nearby river, they looted several Spanish ships, seizing coins, merchandise, and slaves. One Spanish vessel managed to slip away when the *Swan* approached it. The frightened crew maneuvered the ship to shore and fled into the forest. Drake and his pirates boarded the ship and stripped it of everything of value. When the crew returned they found a note, probably written by Drake, taunting them for running away. "Since you will not come courteously to talk with us . . . you will find your [ship] spoiled by your own fault," the note read. It went on to warn that Drake wasn't finished in the Caribbean: "If there be cause, we will be devils rather than men."

A few months later, Drake and his men boarded a mail boat, killed several people, and dumped the mail overboard. Drake's Protestant crew mocked the ship's Catholic friar, stripping him of his clothes and taunting him before sailing off in search of more plunder.

Drake and his crew returned to Plymouth with loot worth about 100,000 English pounds—a very large sum at the time. But even more importantly, he had gathered vital information from his Spanish victims about the route they used to transport their silver and gold home from South America.

The Spanish carried their treasure overland from the mines of the Andes mountains to ports along the Pacific coast. Ships then took the gold and silver north to the Isthmus of Panama—the thin strip of land that separates the Pacific and Atlantic oceans. There, laborers loaded the precious metals on the backs of mules or onto riverboats. They hauled the loot through the jungle to the Caribbean coast, where it was stored in warehouses. Then, once a year, ships arrived to sail the treasure back to Spain.

Drake knew that these vessels traveled across the Atlantic in heavily armed fleets, making them difficult to capture at sea. But he realized that he might be able to intercept the treasure before it reached those ships. A daring plan began to form in the pirate's mind.

CHAPTER 5

Fame and Fortune

DRAKE HITS THE JACKPOT
in the jungles of Panama.

Returning to England in 1571, Drake plotted his next move. Every year, the Spanish piled a fortune in gold and silver into warehouses near the eastern coast of Panama to await the arrival of the Spanish treasure fleet. If Drake attacked the warehouses at just the right time, the loot would be his. He must have dreamed about the treasure so often that he could almost feel the heavy bars of gold and silver in the palms of his hands. Now it was time to turn his dream into real wealth.

In May 1572, Drake departed Plymouth with two small ships. Among the sailors in his crew were his younger brothers John and Joseph. After a swift ocean crossing, Drake anchored his vessels in a secluded bay on the Caribbean coast of Panama. There, he built a small fort and made plans to surprise the Spanish.

But Drake's plans went terribly wrong. The English had arrived in the New World too late to intercept the treasure. The year's haul of gold and silver had already set sail for Spain. The pirates raided the town of Nombre de Dios, where Drake hoped to find some remaining loot. Drake was wounded in the raid. He fainted from the loss of blood and had to be carried back to his ship. For all his trouble, he had found nothing to steal.

From there, things only got worse. Drake's brother John was killed in a failed attack on a Spanish ship. Then Joseph Drake died from a sudden illness—most likely yellow fever, a deadly disease spread by mosquitoes. The outbreak grew worse, killing 27 more crew members.

Now Drake had only 35 or 40 men left.

Drake must have been devastated, but he refused to give up. For more than nine months, he and his starving crew prowled the coast, forming alliances with escaped slaves and joining forces with French sailors who had also come to steal from the Spanish. Finally, in April 1573, the English and French pirates, along with the Africans, went ashore to ambush a mule train.

FRANCIS DRAKE IS CARRIED AWAY after being wounded during a raid. Drake had hoped to steal Spanish gold and silver. Instead, his men were nearly wiped out by Spanish guns and yellow fever.

As Drake approached the convoy, he realized that the long wait was about to pay off. Through the trees he saw 200 mules carrying an enormous load of gold and silver. And the treasure was guarded by just a few tired Spanish soldiers.

Capturing the loot proved to be fairly easy. The Spanish guards did not put up much of a fight. But there was so much loot that Drake and his men couldn't carry it all. They loaded themselves down with gold and buried the silver in the dense forest before heading back to their ships. When they reached the coast, they found a Spanish fleet waiting for them. And their own ships were nowhere to be seen.

Drake quickly built a crude raft out of tree trunks and slipped past the Spanish ships. He took refuge on an island until he was rescued by his fleet. When his men asked how things had gone in the jungle, he just smiled and pulled out a big piece of gold. Then he ordered his men to ready the boats so they could rescue their comrades and collect the buried loot.

ON HIS EXPEDITION to Panama in 1573, Drake caught a
glimpse of the Pacific Ocean. It's likely that he immediately began
to plan pirating expeditions there.

In August 1573, Francis Drake returned to England a wealthy man. He bought a house in Plymouth, as well as more ships. He had become known as an admired sea captain and a respected member of the community. Even his enemies in Spain called him "one of the most skilled mariners in England."

But Francis Drake was already planning an even more audacious expedition. During those long months in the jungles of Panama, he had once climbed to the top of a tree. Behind him was a body of water that he knew like an old friend—the Caribbean Sea. In front of him lay a beautiful stranger, glistening in the sun—the broad waters of the Pacific Ocean.

No Englishman had ever entered the waters of the Pacific. To get there from the Atlantic, a ship would have to sail around the bottom tip of South America. It was a long and dangerous trip. Only the Spanish and the Portuguese had done it; only they knew how.

Francis Drake swore he would be the next man to attempt this perilous journey.

PART 2

Around the World

~~~~~~~~~~~~~~~~

Big Plans

THE MARINER SETS OFF ON
A SECRET MISSION
to the far corners of the map.

It took Francis Drake four years to put his bold scheme into action. The expedition to the Pacific Ocean would be a huge and expensive project. Drake must have spent many weeks in London, courting the richest, most powerful members of the English nobility. Many of them ended up investing in the venture. Even Drake's former mentor, John Hawkins, contributed money. And Queen Elizabeth herself offered Drake a royal ship to use on the journey.

The expedition was wrapped in secrecy, and its exact purpose is still unclear. Most likely, Drake's primary aim was piracy. He probably had his eye on the shiploads of gold and silver the Spanish sent up the Pacific coast to Panama. Drake suspected that the Spanish would never expect an attack that far from Europe—so their ports

DRAKE CONVINCED QUEEN ELIZABETH to fund his expedition to the Pacific Ocean. The queen needed cash to fight the Catholic enemies who surrounded her country. So she offered him a ship in exchange for a share of the profits.

FRANCIS DRAKE PREPARES to sail from Plymouth
Sound to the Pacific coast of South America, where he probably
hoped to rob undefended Spanish ports.

along the Pacific coast would be poorly defended. If he could just reach the waters of the Pacific, he might become rich beyond his wildest dreams.

In December 1577, a crew of 170 men readied five ships at Plymouth Sound for Drake's expedition. Drake was to command a vessel armed with 18 cannons—and he intended to use them.

Before Drake left, Queen Elizabeth told him that she would "gladly be revenged on the king of Spain," who had become her fierce political and religious rival. Philip wanted to stamp out the Protestant revolution and restore the Catholic faith all across Europe. In 1571, English spies had uncovered a plot to murder Elizabeth and place her Catholic cousin, Mary Queen of Scots, on the throne. Spanish officials had been deeply involved in the scheme.

Elizabeth wanted to punish King Philip and Spain, and she told Francis Drake that he was "the only man who might do this exploit." But neither the pirate nor his queen knew just how big the task would be.

CHAPTER 7

Mutiny and Murder

Getting on Drake's bad side proves to be A SERIOUS MISTAKE.

On DECEMBER 13, 1577, DRAKE SAILED FROM Plymouth with the queen's blessing. His probable mission: To surprise the Spanish on the Pacific coast of South America, strike a blow for Protestant England, and return home loaded down with loot.

After a safe voyage south from England, Drake's fleet reached the coast of North Africa on Christmas morning of 1577. Drake dispatched a small ship to search for plunder. In January, his men seized three Spanish fishing boats and four Portuguese vessels. Drake added the captured ships to his growing fleet.

Aboard one of the Portuguese ships, Drake found a mariner named Nuno De Silva. De Silva was a skilled pilot, adept at steering ships through difficult waters. He claimed to be familiar with the coast of South America. He also owned an excellent set of maps. Drake decided that De Silva could be a useful guide through these unknown waters. Drake freed the rest of the Portuguese crew but kept the pilot as a prisoner on his ship, the *Pelican*.

Drake treated De Silva well. He often invited the pilot to dine with him in his private quarters. De Silva was impressed with the luxuries Drake allowed himself on the crowded ship. The food arrived on silver dishes, and musicians played throughout the meal.

De Silva was also impressed with Drake himself, whom he described as short, stout, and strong, with a reddish complexion. Drake, he wrote later, was a "great mariner." He added that the English commander was a very religious man who led Protestant services aboard ship.

During their dinners together, De Silva won Drake's respect. At least one other member of the expedition was not so fortunate.

Thomas Doughty, a well-educated nobleman, began the voyage as a friend of Drake's. Doughty had invested money in the expedition. He captained one of the ships and was popular with the crew. According to one account, he and Drake were "equal companions" in the venture.

But somewhere in the middle of the ocean, Drake turned against Doughty. The conflict probably started when Doughty accused Drake's brother Thomas of stealing loot from a captured Portuguese ship. The friendship quickly disintegrated. Drake accused Doughty of challenging his authority and called him a traitor. Drake even claimed that Doughty had used magic to bring bad weather upon the expedition.

FRANCIS DRAKE (center) with the severed head of
Thomas Doughty. The two men were supposed to be equal
partners, but Drake accused Doughty of treason and sorcery
and had him executed.

In June 1578, the fleet dropped anchor at Port Saint Julian, a harbor near the southern tip of South America. Drake announced that he was putting Doughty on trial for mutiny. He ordered everyone ashore on a sandy island just off the coast, where he assembled a jury to decide Doughty's fate. Drake claimed he had a document from the queen giving him authority to hold such a trial. But he never showed that document to anyone, and it's probable that the whole proceeding was illegal. Nonetheless, the members of the jury did not dare go against their commander's wishes. They voted Thomas Doughty guilty as charged.

Two days later, Doughty knelt before the executioner's block. The sharp, shiny blade swung down upon his neck. Then Francis Drake lifted the severed head to show his sailors. "This is the end of traitors," he declared.

For years after Thomas Doughty's death, the question would linger: Had those sailors just seen an act of justice——or a cold-blooded murder?

CHAPTER 8

Through the Strait

The mariner goes WHERE NO ENGLISHMAN HAS DARED TO SAIL.

HAVING DISPATCHED HIS RIVAL IN ruthless fashion, Drake turned to the next obstacle facing the tiny fleet: the Strait of Magellan. Located at the southernmost tip of South America, this narrow strip of freezing water leads from the Atlantic Ocean to the Pacific. In Drake's time, it struck terror into the hearts of sailors.

The strait was infamous for its deadly winds, dangerous currents, and dense fogs. It zigzagged between sheer cliffs that offered ships no place to land if they got into trouble. The people who lived nearby were rumored to be fierce giants.

The strait was named after the famous Portuguese sea captain Ferdinand Magellan. While working for the king of Spain in 1520, Magellan had become the first

A CRUDE MAP of the mysterious Strait of Magellan. The strait was a maze of icy water channels and rocky cliffs—and the watery grave of hundreds of Spanish sailors. No English ship had ever made the crossing.

mariner to make it through the perilous waterway. Since then, only a few other Spanish explorers had attempted the journey. They did not have much luck. The Strait of Magellan had already destroyed many ships and claimed the lives of hundreds of sailors.

Drake did not dare to enter the strait in July—the coldest month of the year in that part of the world. So he and his men set up camp at Port Saint Julian and waited for the weather to improve. By the time they were ready to try their luck, only three vessels were in good enough condition to make the trip.

Drake's three weather-beaten ships sailed into the waterway in late August 1578. The pilots had to make their way carefully because they did not have good maps. Nonetheless, they made the 350-mile voyage in just two weeks. Francis Drake had arrived in the Pacific Ocean at last.

The commander had no time to celebrate. As soon as the expedition entered the Pacific, the ships were blasted by wild winds, snow, and hail. More storms followed. One fierce gale separated the smallest of the three vessels from the other two. No one ever saw the ship again. Another storm blew the two remaining ships apart. Lost in a thick fog, the ships never reunited. Drake later learned that the captain of the other vessel had decided to give up. He sailed back through the strait and eventually made it home to England.

Now Drake and the crew of the *Pelican* were on their own in a vast and stormy sea. But the commander had no intention of turning back. He began to sail up the Pacific coast of South America. On November 25, 1578, his ship reached an island off the coast of modern-day Chile. Drake and some of his men went ashore to get wood and fresh water. There, they were ambushed by local villagers. Two sailors were wounded, one of whom later died. Another two were captured and never seen again. Drake himself survived arrow wounds to his head.

It had now been almost a year since the expedition left England. So far, the pirate had very little to show for his troubles. But Drake's luck was about to change.

CHAPTER 9

Loose in the Pacific

Let the MAYHEM AND MARAUDING BEGIN.

ON DECEMBER 5, 1578, DRAKE TOOK THE *Pelican* into harbor at the South American town of Valparaiso. There, he came upon a Spanish ship named *La Capitana*. Realizing that this could be a big prize, he sent 18 soldiers in a small boat to raid the Spanish ship.

The crew of *La Capitana* prepared to greet the approaching sailors as friends and countrymen. They had no reason to assume the newcomers were anything but Spaniards. They had never seen a foreign ship in this part of the world. They beat a drum in welcome and readied a cask of wine.

But when the boat pulled alongside *La Capitana*, one of the strangers leaped aboard and hit the pilot in the face. "Get below, you dog!" he shouted. The rest of Drake's men swarmed onto the ship and quickly overwhelmed its crew. One Spaniard jumped into the water and swam away. The others were locked up on a lower deck.

Francis Drake's pirate raids in the Pacific had begun.

Drake and his men discovered a stash of wine, some lumber, and four large chests full of gold aboard *La Capitana*. They loaded up their boat and rowed the booty back to the *Pelican*. Then the raiding party went ashore and attacked the town. They took whatever treasure they could get their hands on and ransacked the Catholic church. Then they sailed off in search of more loot.

For the next several months, Drake moved slowly up the coast, terrorizing Spanish colonists and filling the hold of the *Pelican* with an enormous amount of loot. He boarded several more ships and invaded a number of towns. In many of his raids, Drake took prisoners and tried to get information out of them. The question was always the same: Where is the silver and gold? If a captive refused to talk, Drake might threaten to cut off his head. Sometimes he had his victims tied up and dropped into the sea.

On March 1, 1579, Drake was cruising off the coast of modern-day Ecuador when he spotted a big Spanish ship in the distance. He had his pilot guide the *Pelican* through the darkening night toward the ship. By 9 P.M., the pirates had pulled up alongside their prey.

Drake ordered the Spanish ship to lower its sails.

"Come and do it yourself," shouted the captain.

With that, Drake's men opened fire with a hail of small artillery and arrows, one of which wounded the Spanish commander. The English pirates poured onto the ship, overwhelming its crew and forcing their captain to surrender.

The pirates were stunned by what they found on board—80 pounds of gold and 13 or 14 chests filled with silver coins. The haul was so big that it took the men six days to transfer all of it to their own vessel. Drake finally had the treasure that would make the entire voyage a grand success.

By now, news of Drake's daring exploits had spread up the coast of South America to Panama and Mexico. Worried Spanish officials wondered where the pirate would strike next. Figuring he might attack the Mexican port of Acapulco, they prepared for a fight.

But Drake never arrived in Acapulco. Nor did he turn around and sail back toward the Strait of Magellan. Instead, he decided to do something no Englishman had

DRAKE AND HIS MEN bombard Spanish ships off the coast of South America. During these raids, the English seized silver and gold, wine, timber, and maps they would need to navigate the Pacific Ocean.

ever done before. He would take his ship all the way around the world.

It's possible that this had been Drake's plan from the start. He had brought a book with him that described the only successful effort to circle the globe—Ferdinand Magellan's famous journey of 1517 to 1522.

But it's also possible that Drake's daring plan was a last-minute decision. The pirate must have known that Spanish ships were now searching for him up and down the coast. Trying to sail back to the strait would be dangerous. Trying to make it through those deadly channels again could be an even greater risk.

One final factor may have affected his decision. In March 1579, Drake captured a ship off the coast of Costa Rica. Onboard he found a collection of Spanish maps of the Pacific Ocean. They were just what he needed for a trip around the world.

The Long Way Home

Drake pulls off an
ALMOST IMPOSSIBLE FEAT.

Francis drake had no idea what might await him in the vast Pacific Ocean. All he knew was that he would have to sail thousands of miles before reaching the nearest land.

Before heading out to sea, Drake needed to ready the *Pelican* for the journey. He sailed north and stopped at a bay along the coast of North America, possibly near modern-day San Francisco. He and his men stayed there for more than a month, cleaning, repairing, and re-supplying the ship. Drake named the place Nova Albion, which is Latin for New England.

Drake and his men left the shores of North America in July or August 1579. They sailed for more than two

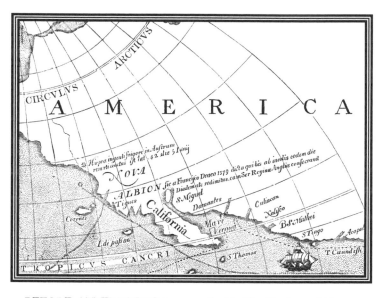

BEFORE ATTEMPTING to cross the Pacific, Drake and his men spent a month repairing and re-supplying the *Pelican* in a harbor on the west coast of North America. Drake named the harbor Nova Albion and claimed it as a colony for England.

months before reaching a tiny island in the western Pacific. A large group of islanders paddled out to greet them in bright red dugout canoes. At first the islanders offered the Englishmen fish in return for beads. Before long they started helping themselves to the sailors' possessions. One of them grabbed a knife and refused to return it. A fight broke out between the two sides, and Drake erupted in anger, ordering his men to fire cannons at the canoes. When the barrage stopped, 20 islanders were dead. Drake left them with one final insult: He named the place the Island of Thieves.

The expedition sailed on. Drake stopped in the Moluccas—islands that were famous for their rare and delicious spices. But when he set out to sea again, disaster struck. The *Pelican* floated into unexpectedly shallow water and ran into a reef. The men tried to free the vessel. But no matter what they did, it would not budge. It looked as though the ship might be stranded forever.

Onboard the *Pelican*, a minister named Francis Fletcher held a religious service for the crew. According to one account of the incident, Fletcher told the men that God was angry with them. He claimed they had been stranded as punishment for their evil deeds, which apparently included the murder of Thomas Doughty. Fletcher told the men to prepare themselves to die.

As it turned out, the minister had been overly pessimistic. The wind suddenly changed direction, and the ship floated back into open water. When it was clear the *Pelican* was out of danger, Drake exploded at Fletcher. He put the minister in chains and threatened to have him hanged. Drake also forced Fletcher wear a sign on his arm labeling him "falsest knave"—the biggest liar—who ever lived.

Drake's men made it through the rest of the journey without mishap. The *Pelican* crossed the Indian Ocean, the great body of water that lies between Australia and Africa. Then it cruised around the southern coast of Africa and headed back toward England. Drake feared

DRAKE RETURNS IN TRIUMPH to Plymouth Sound. He had circled the globe, struck fear into the Spanish, and made vast profits for himself, his queen, and his other investors.

that Spanish ships would try to stop him before he could get home with his treasure. But no enemy vessels ever appeared on the horizon.

On September 26, 1580, Francis Drake sailed into Plymouth Sound. He had traveled more than 30,000 miles. It had taken him almost three years. But he had made history—and he had made himself rich. Now he was home at last.

Sir Francis Drake in Pictures

DRAWN TO THE SEA

Francis Drake (right) was the son of a minister who may also have been a horse thief. When Drake was a teenager, he moved to the port city of Plymouth. He spent the rest of his life there or at sea.

THE ART OF PIRACY

Drake was a relative of William Hawkins, the richest merchant in Plymouth. William's son John (left) was a pirate, brave but cruel. John taught Drake how to navigate the seas and chase down foreign ships.

AN EVIL TRADE

Drake and Hawkins rounded up Africans "partly by the sword and partly by other means" and sailed them across the Atlantic to be sold to Spanish colonists.

DESERTER OR SURVIVOR?

While returning home from a slave-trading expedition, Drake and Hawkins were caught in a hurricane. They were then ambushed by the Spanish. Drake deserted Hawkins the night after the battle.

WHATEVER IT TAKES

Queen Elizabeth's England was a small Protestant nation surrounded by hostile Catholic powers. The country had no overseas colonies and was poorer than its enemies. Elizabeth began to rely on Drake's raids to fund her army and navy.

PAIN AND PLUNDER

In 1572, Drake and his crew sailed to Panama in search of Spanish gold. After epidemics and failed raids, the pirates struck it rich when they came across a mule train carrying an enormous load of gold and silver.

NEW HORIZON

Drake first saw the Pacific Ocean from the jungles of Panama. He vowed to sail there and rob unsuspecting Spanish ports.

DIRE STRAITS

The only way to sail to the Pacific from the Atlantic was through the deadly Strait of Magellan, a jumble of sheer cliffs and icy water channels.

LOST IN THE NEW WORLD

After Drake and his crew made it through the Strait of Magellan, the pirates had to survive fierce storms, native ambushes, Spanish warships, and vast stretches of open, unexplored ocean.

RAGS TO RICHES

As Drake sailed around the world, he looted chests full of gold, silver, pearls, and precious stones—a treasure worth the equivalent of about 23 tons of gold. The plunder made Drake one of the richest men in England.

BANKROLLING A NATION

Queen Elizabeth's share of the profits from Drake's pirating allowed her to pay off England's debts. The queen honored Drake by knighting him.

HOLY WARRIOR

King Philip II of Spain believed God required him to restore all of Europe to Catholicism. He spent years planning to invade England.

IN THE RED

Drake's ships attacked the Spanish colony of Santo Domingo in 1586. During this expedition, Drake lost 750 of his men. The expedition failed to make a profit.

A RAID ON SPAIN
In 1587, Elizabeth learned of Philip's plan to invade England and sent Drake to raid the Spanish mainland.

ENGLAND IS SAVED
English galleons attack the Spanish Armada, which has formed a defensive crescent. The Armada was battered to pieces by superior English firepower and left to founder in the stormy North Sea.

OUT WITH A WHIMPER
Drake is buried at sea after a last failed raid. In his prime, he was the most famous and feared pirate on earth.

PART 3

From Pirate to Knight

Drake becomes a
16TH-CENTURY SUPERSTAR.

A HUGE CROWD GATHERED AT THE ROYAL
shipyard on the Thames River in London. It was April
4, 1581—half a year since Drake had returned to
England—and Queen Elizabeth herself was about to
honor the man who had sailed around the world.

The pirate had become a national hero. Even his
ship, now renamed the *Golden Hind*, was famous. It had
been scrubbed clean and covered with fancy decorations

for the occasion. Festive banners waved from its masts. Rich nobles wearing priceless jewels and expensive clothes waited anxiously to climb on deck.

The crowd pressed close to catch a glimpse of the queen. Even the gangway leading to the ship was packed with people. After Elizabeth walked across, the bridge collapsed. About 100 people fell into the mud.

On the ship, Drake hosted a lavish banquet. When everyone had eaten, the queen told him to kneel before her. Then she took out a sword. She said that the king of Spain was so angry with Drake that he was demanding the pirate's head. "Now," she joked, "I have a golden sword to strike it off."

Instead, the queen handed the weapon to an official next to her. He touched the sword lightly on Drake's shoulders. With this act, the pirate was transformed into a knight—one of England's highest honors. From now on, the world would know him not as Francis Drake, but as Sir Francis Drake.

Few men of Drake's modest background had ever

THIS ILLUSTRATION SHOWS Elizabeth knighting Sir Francis Drake. In reality, she had another official perform the ceremony.

been granted a knighthood. But few men had ever accomplished such astonishing feats. Drake had sailed around the world, humbled the mighty Spanish, and brought home a fortune in plunder. Even after giving much of the loot to the queen and his other investors, Drake was one of the richest men in England.

More honors and big changes followed in the

months to come. Drake became mayor of Plymouth and a Member of Parliament—the highest lawmaking body in England. Two years after the ceremony in London, Drake's wife, Mary, died. A couple of years later, he found another bride—the young, beautiful, and wealthy Elizabeth Sydenham. Together, they lived in Buckland Abbey, an old church that had been transformed into a stunning, three-story mansion.

Drake, too, had been transformed. Once a lowly sailor trying to make his way on the rough docks of Plymouth, he had turned himself into a respected nobleman.

Nonetheless, some people still saw Sir Francis Drake as a common criminal. One of those people was John Doughty, the brother of the man Drake had beheaded during his round-the-world journey. When Drake became a knight, John Doughty erupted in anger. He insisted that the queen was honoring "the arrantest knave, the vilest villain, the falsest thief, and the cruelest murderer that ever was born."

Doughty insisted that Drake be put on trial for the murder of his brother. Nothing ever came of his demand. But in 1582, John Doughty was himself tossed into prison. A man named Patrick Mason had confessed under torture to working as a Spanish spy and implicated Doughty in his schemes. According to Mason, the Spanish government had offered Doughty a huge sum of money to kill or kidnap Francis Drake.

Doughty may or may not have taken the money. But the fact that it was offered makes it clear that after two decades prowling the seas, Drake had become one of the most hated men in Spain. Spanish sailors feared nothing more than the sight of Drake's masts on the horizon. They called the English pirate *El Draque*, which meant "The Dragon" or "The Devil."

For now, the Dragon was content to remain on land. Unfortunately for Spain, the beast would grow hungry again.

Back to
the New World

DISEASE AND BAD LUCK
plague Drake on his return to
the Caribbean.

In SEPTEMBER 1585, FRANCIS DRAKE SET OFF
on another expedition to the Americas. The voyage
came at a crucial time. Spain and England were edging
closer to war with each passing day.

Spain's King Philip II made no secret of his hatred
for Queen Elizabeth. The Protestant queen had done
nothing to stop Drake and other English pirates, and

Philip was furious. In May 1585, he concluded that he needed more vessels to guard against raids on Spanish shipping. So he ordered his troops to seize all English, Dutch, and German ships at Spanish ports. Up and down the coast, Spanish soldiers boarded foreign vessels and declared them to be the property of the Spanish crown.

For Queen Elizabeth, that was the last straw. She decided to drop all attempts to maintain friendly relations with Spain. In September 1585, she dispatched Drake to the New World with a fleet of more than 20 ships.

Drake's plan was to raid Spanish towns in the Caribbean. If the raids went well, he would leave troops in at least one of those towns, giving the English a permanent base in the region. And if everything went as planned, he would finally capture the treasure fleet as it made its annual voyage to Spain.

But on this trip, nothing went according to plan. On his way to the Caribbean, Drake learned that the treasure fleet had slipped past several weeks earlier. Even worse, a terrible sickness began to spread through the ships. It left sailors with raging fevers and spots on their skin—possible symptoms of typhus, a killer disease sometimes known as "ship fever." About 300 men died before the expedition even reached the New World.

Drake's first target in the Caribbean was Santo Domingo, where his men made the raid that sent residents fleeing for the hills. Drake demanded a million ducats—a pile of gold coins that would have weighed nearly four tons. The city's leaders could come up with only 25,000 ducats.

The same thing happened in Cartagena, a port city on the Spanish Main. Drake burned down 248 houses, but he received a ransom of only 107,000 ducats. He had hoped to get much more.

Drake wanted to attack more towns, but his men continued to fall sick and die. "Every day, they were throwing corpses overboard," an escaped Spanish

A 16TH-CENTURY ILLUSTRATION of Drake's invasion of Cartagena. Drake's men burned down more than 200 houses and demanded loot from the Spanish.

prisoner later reported. In the spring of 1586, a frustrated Francis Drake decided to head back for England. About 750 of his men were dead, most of them from disease. And he had not even plundered enough treasure to cover the cost of the expedition.

A VISIT TO VIRGINIA

DRAKE'S RAID ON THE CARIBBEAN WASN'T
the only English expedition to the New World in 1585.
In April of that year, seven ships left Plymouth to
start the first English settlement in the future United
States—a colony the settlers called Virginia.

That summer, they built a fort on Roanoke Island in
what is now North Carolina. But the settlement quickly
fell apart. They ran out of food and fought with local
Native Americans. Then, just when it looked as if things
could not get worse, a mysterious fleet of ships arrived.

At first the colonists thought the Spanish had come to
wipe them out. But the ships belonged to Francis Drake,
on his way back to England
after his raids in the
Caribbean. Drake claimed
he had come to save the
settlers from the Spanish.
He took the starving
people aboard and sailed
them safely home.

THE FIRST ROANOKE
settlement survived one year.

CHAPTER 13

Attack on Spain

Drake hits his enemy
WHERE IT HURTS THE MOST.

F RANCIS DRAKE RETURNED TO PLYMOUTH
in late July 1586. He brought some treasure, but not
nearly as much as everyone expected. For Queen
Elizabeth and other sponsors of the expedition, the
pirate's raids in the Caribbean were a disappointment.

Nonetheless, Drake had succeeded in spreading
terror. Not only had he destroyed a number of key
Spanish towns, he had exposed the vulnerability
of Spain's empire in the Americas. And he had added
to his reputation in Spain as a dreaded figure who

seemed capable of fighting a one-man war against King Philip. Rumors ran wild about where he would strike next. Even the head of the Catholic Church in Rome took notice of the Protestant pirate. "God only knows what he may succeed in doing!" said Pope Sixtus V.

By the time Drake returned from the Caribbean, King Philip was already preparing a plan to force not only the pirate but all of Protestant England into submission. In April 1586, the king gave orders to begin preparing a huge fleet—the Spanish Armada. The Armada had a fateful mission: Secure the English Channel while an invasion force of thousands of Spanish troops was ferried from the Netherlands to England.

The king meant to keep his ambitious scheme a secret. But such a huge undertaking proved impossible to hide from English spies. Before long, news of the Spanish Armada got back to Queen Elizabeth. She began preparing her country for war.

Once again, the queen called on the services of Sir Francis Drake. He was anxious to help. Drake knew that if the Armada succeeded, the Spanish conquerors would bring Catholicism back to England. He saw the upcoming war as a battle of good against evil. King Philip, he claimed, was the enemy of God.

On April 2, 1587, Drake set sail with a fleet of 24 ships and about 3,000 men. He headed straight for Spain. His goal was to strike at the enemy before the Armada set sail. He might not be able to destroy the Spanish fleet, but at least he could delay it.

On April 19, Drake arrived at the Spanish port of Cádiz. The harbor was full of ships loading supplies for the Armada. Drake descended on the unsuspecting vessels with "more speed and arrogance than any pirate has ever shown," in the words of a Spanish observer. The attackers captured four ships, sank several others, and torched about 30 more. They left the harbor so full of smoke and flames that to one Spaniard it "seemed like a huge volcano, or something out of Hell." Drake's men also managed to destroy all the seasoned wood the Spanish had set aside to make storage barrels for the Armada.

Next, the English fleet headed for the Portuguese coast. Philip had conquered Portugal in 1580, so the region now belonged to Spain. Drake sent 1,000 troops ashore at the ancient port of Lagos. The Spanish fought them off, killing many of the attackers. But the English had better luck at the nearby town of Sagres. Drake's Protestant marauders took special pleasure in destroying a Catholic monastery. "They committed their usual feasts and drunkenness, their diabolical rampages and obscenities," concluded one Spanish report. "They stole everything they found and then set the place on fire."

Drake had one more "obscenity" for the Spaniards. In June, his fleet surrounded a Spanish royal ship in the Atlantic. Its cargo included spices, silks, velvets, gold, and jewels. Drake captured the lavish prize and set sail for home.

QUEEN ELIZABETH SENT DRAKE to attack the coast
of Spain and delay Philip's invasion of England. Drake destroyed
dozens of Spain's warships and supposedly bragged that he had
singed the Spanish king's beard.

Back in England, Drake turned his attention to a more personal matter—a bitter grudge against an officer named William Borough. An experienced sea captain, Borough had begun the expedition as Drake's second-in-command, but the two men quickly began to quarrel. Borough thought that some of Drake's actions during the raids on Portugal and Spain were rash and dangerous. During the journey, he accused his commander of putting the lives of the men at risk just to bring glory to his own name. This made Drake furious. He promptly stripped Borough of his command. Borough's ship later left the fleet and sailed home early.

Drake accused Borough of cowardice, mutiny, and desertion. Borough was able to beat the charges in court. He insisted that by remaining with Drake he would have "assuredly been put to death"—just as Thomas Doughty had been on the frigid, lonely coast of South America. And he reminded the court that back in 1568, Drake had abandoned his own commanding officer and sailed for home. Did the pirate now "altogether forget" that he had left John Hawkins to fend for himself in Mexico?

Francis Drake could never quite escape the past. Despite his success, some people still thought of him as a coward. Drake would soon give his critics more evidence to fuel their suspicions.

CHAPTER 14

Against the Armada

DRAKE'S CONDUCT UNDER FIRE is called into question.

"THERE WAS NEVER ANY FORCE SO strong as [the one] now . . . making ready against your Majesty," Drake warned Queen Elizabeth in April 1588. One month later, the mighty Spanish Armada was ready to sail. The vast fleet contained an astonishing 130 ships staffed by 8,000 sailors. The warships also carried 19,000 soldiers, specially trained to board enemy ships and seize them in hand-to-hand combat.

After his raid on Spain the previous year, Drake had urged the queen to prepare "strongly." Elizabeth was reluctant to go further into debt, but on her orders warships were cleaned, repaired, and refitted. Soon, the English boasted a force of 120 ships armed with cannons that could fire farther and more accurately than any in the Armada.

The English also fielded many talented mariners. Leading the fleet was the head of the English navy, Lord Charles Howard. Drake served as his vice admiral, or second-in-command. Among the other captains was Drake's mentor, John Hawkins, now about 55 years old.

ELIZABETH PUT LORD HOWARD in charge of England's naval defense. He struggled to control his impulsive second-in-command, Sir Francis Drake.

The English commanders braced themselves for a battle to the death with the Armada. But even before the Spanish fleet reached England, it found itself in trouble. In June, the Spaniards ran into a terrible storm and had to take shelter in northern Spain. By that time, food supplies were already running low. The Duke of Medina-Sidonia, admiral of the Spanish Armada, begged his king to call off the attack. But Philip had gone too far to back down. "I have dedicated this enterprise to God," the king wrote to Sidonia. "Pull yourself together . . . and do your part!"

On July 19, news reached Plymouth that the Armada had been spotted off the English coast. Drake and his fellow officers boarded their ships and headed out to sea in search of the Spanish.

By the dawn of July 21, the two fleets were poised for battle. They traded shots off the coast of Plymouth. The Spanish captains tried to move in and cut off one or two English ships so they could send their soldiers swarming aboard. Drake and Howard kept their distance, using their superior firing range to their advantage. After several hours of fighting, the Spanish ships broke off and sailed up the English Channel toward the invasion force waiting on the coast of the Netherlands.

Howard gave Drake the honor of leading the pursuit. Drake hung a large lantern burning at the rear of his ship to guide the English fleet through the night. But when his countrymen looked for the beacon, all they saw were dark seas. Drake had put out the lantern and slipped away.

Sir Francis Drake, the fearless protector of England, had spotted a Spanish ship damaged from a collision after the battle. His instincts as a pirate took over and he deserted his command in search of loot. As it happened, the damaged ship was carrying pay for Spanish troops. Drake nabbed a large amount of gold and several enemy officers to hold for ransom.

When the fleet regrouped, Drake and other commanders harassed the Armada as it made its way up the English Channel. On July 29, near the Flemish coast, they attacked the Spanish fleet in force. Blasting away at close range, their guns created so much smoke that the Armada's commander, Admiral Sidonia, had to climb his mast to find an escape route. The English sunk or captured at least four Spanish vessels that day and seriously damaged many more.

Most of the Armada drifted to the north, abandoning the invasion plans. The dejected Spanish captains had no choice but to make a long and dangerous journey into the North Sea, circling around Scotland and Ireland before heading home. During the course of the trip, dozens more Spanish ships foundered or ran aground.

The Armada disaster proved to be one of the worst defeats in naval history. Of the 130 vessels that had embarked for England, only 60 are known to have made it safely back to Spain. As many as 15,000 Spaniards died at sea during the ill-fated expedition. Without protection from the Armada, the Spanish army in the Netherlands had to call off its invasion.

For England, the campaign was an unqualified

THE ENGLISH (RIGHT) SENT FIRESHIPS to scatter Spanish
warships and drive them from the port of Calais, where they were
anchored. After the Armada regrouped, it was severely battered at the
Battle of Gravelines and forced to retreat into the stormy North Sea.

success. Queen Elizabeth celebrated her triumph over
King Philip. All across the country, people rejoiced.

But at least one small dark cloud hung over the
victory—Francis Drake's conduct under fire. Hadn't
the vice admiral abandoned his duties to chase down a
gold-laden Spanish ship? Drake's rash and selfish act in

the heat of battle enraged many of his fellow officers. They accused their commander of pursuing plunder over patriotism. The famous explorer and naval captain Martin Frobisher insisted that Drake had revealed himself to be either "a cowardly knave or a traitor."

Francis Drake did not know it yet, but his glory days were already behind him. His reputation at home—and his fortunes at sea—had begun to sink.

PART 4

Final
Voyages

CHAPTER 15

Invasion of Portugal

Drake loses his cool
AND SHOWS HIS AGE.

THE PIRATE WAS NOT FEELING WELL. AT some point in 1588, he had injured himself fighting a fire in his London home. Now the pain had grown unbearable. He told a friend that he was "unable to stand without much grief."

He was almost 50 years old—ancient by the standards of his time. Men in London's poorer areas typically died between the ages of 20 and 25. In the richer parts of town, they survived to be 30 or 35. Only the wealthiest, strongest, and luckiest people lived into their forties and beyond.

Drake had been all three of those things. But his strength and luck were beginning to give out. He had survived countless battles. He had escaped deadly epidemics. Luck and quick thinking had saved him from a hundred difficult situations. Nonetheless, time was finally catching up with him. He no longer felt invincible.

Still, as one of England's top naval commanders, Drake had no time to take it easy. The Spanish Armada had been defeated, but Spain remained a formidable rival for control of the seas. Queen Elizabeth wanted to make sure the Spanish navy could never attack England again. In April 1589, a massive English fleet cruised out of Plymouth Sound. It included more than 150 vessels and as many as 23,000 men—the largest naval force ever to leave England. At the head of this mighty fighting force was the famous Francis Drake.

The mission had a number of goals—none of them easy. The first goal was to raid ports in Spain and Portugal and destroy all the Spanish warships they could find. The second was to invade Portugal. This once-powerful country had been under Spanish control since 1580. Now Queen Elizabeth hoped to install a king loyal to herself. A third aim of the expedition was to capture the Azores—a group of Spanish-owned islands 1,000 miles west of Portugal. The English wanted the islands as a base for raids on the Spanish treasure fleets.

Drake had tackled many difficult assignments before—often with stunning success. This time, he wasn't up to the task. Queen Elizabeth wanted, first and foremost, to cripple the Spanish navy. With that in mind, she had ordered Drake to attack the busy harbor of Santander in northern Spain, where many warships were stationed. Drake ignored the order. Instead, he attacked the town of La Coruna, where he found only a few vessels. Then he went off in search of wealthy merchant ships to plunder.

Drake then headed toward Lisbon, the Portuguese capital. Before he arrived, disease had spread through his fleet, weakening or killing hundreds of sailors.

In May, the English converged on Lisbon by land and sea. Drake landed a force of foot soldiers and sent them marching south toward the capital. He took the English fleet down the coast, promising to pound the city with artillery shells from the harbor. But when the time came, Drake hesitated. Instead of attacking Lisbon, he kept his ships at the mouth of a nearby river. True, the winds weren't perfect. And true, many of his men were sick and weak. It would have been risky to go ahead with the attack. But risks had never stopped Drake before. In his old age, the commander was losing confidence.

The raid on Lisbon failed miserably, leading Drake to abandon the mission and sail for home. The expedition had wasted huge amounts of money. It had cost between 4,000 and 10,000 men their lives. In the end it accomplished nothing.

Queen Elizabeth was furious with Drake. She told him that he had disobeyed her direct orders and could expect to be treated as a traitor. Drake was forced to sit through a long interrogation by the queen's Privy Council. He was never punished, but his reputation was badly damaged.

For years, Sir Francis Drake had been a national hero. Now, even some of his longtime supporters began to wonder whether his best days were behind him.

One Last Disaster

A reunion with
an old friend
TURNS FATAL.

SIX YEARS PASSED BEFORE FRANCIS DRAKE
sailed for his country again. He spent much of that
time trying to improve fortifications in his hometown
of Plymouth. Drake wanted to make sure that the
port was protected against Spanish raids.

The old mariner threw himself into this effort. But
he missed the sea. He wanted one more chance to battle
the Spanish—and to repair the reputation that had
been so damaged during the failed raid on Lisbon.

Drake's opportunity finally came in 1595, when Queen Elizabeth decided it was time once again to harass the Spanish in the Caribbean. But even then, the queen did not give Drake complete control of the expedition. She no longer trusted the wayward naval commander. She wanted another sea captain along to make sure Drake followed her wishes.

The mariner she chose for the job was John Hawkins. Thanks to the queen, Drake and the man who taught him how to be a pirate 40 years earlier were reunited for one last voyage. Elizabeth gave them equal authority over the expedition. The two mariners would each get a third of any treasure they could capture. The queen would get the rest.

Drake and Hawkins sailed from Plymouth Sound on August 28, 1595, with a fleet of 27 ships. Both men had plenty of experience in the Caribbean. What they did not know was how much the region had changed in recent years. After suffering through countless raids by Drake and other pirates, the Spanish had beefed up fortifications at their American outposts. They had also built faster ships for the treasure fleet and placed it under heavier guard.

The two old mariners who sailed into the Atlantic that fall were ill equipped to handle their new and improved rivals. Hawkins was in his 60s. Drake was about 55. Neither man was in shape to weather the long and exhausting journey across the Atlantic. But age wasn't their only problem. Drake and Hawkins just didn't get along. Hawkins was cautious and careful. Drake was impulsive. On their last journey to the New World together, he had made a sudden decision to abandon Hawkins. No doubt Hawkins had not forgotten Drake's betrayal.

It wasn't long before the two men started to argue. Drake wanted to raid an island in the Canaries, off the coast of Africa. Hawkins thought the plan was a waste of time. Drake forged ahead, and the attack turned into a complete failure. More than 40 Englishmen died for nothing.

More bad news followed. After crossing the Atlantic, two small English ships lagged behind the fleet in the eastern Caribbean. One of them fell into enemy hands, and its crew told the Spanish where Drake and Hawkins were headed—the island of Puerto Rico.

Before Drake and Hawkins reached their destination, tragedy struck again. On October 31, 1595, John Hawkins fell sick. Within days, he was so ill that he couldn't leave his bed. On November 12, with the fleet anchored off San Juan, Puerto Rico, the old pirate and slave trader died.

If Drake grieved over the loss of his partner, he left no record of his feelings. In any event, the Spanish gave him little time for regret. Before the crew could arrange Hawkins's burial at sea, a fleet of Spanish warships opened fire on the English ships. The fierce battle left as many as 400 Englishmen dead.

Drake reluctantly decided to abandon the attack on Puerto Rico. He assured his men that there were "twenty places far more wealthy and easier to be gotten."

DRAKE'S MEN STRUGGLE through a swamp during their failed invasion of Panama. Once the greatest pirate in the world, Drake seemed to have run out of luck. In raid after raid, he led his men headlong into disaster.

Drake soon discovered that nothing would be easy on this voyage. Less than ten years earlier, he had ransacked Cartagena on the Spanish Main. Now he found the city heavily defended. He decided not to even attempt an attack.

Instead, he sailed to Panama. Back in 1573, Panama had been the site of one of Drake's greatest raids. Now he sent his men into the jungles again, hoping to capture the key port of Panama City on the Pacific coast. This time, the Spanish fought them off.

The expedition had met with an endless string of failures. Drake became depressed. He was accustomed to raiding undefended ports and making easy profits in the New World. Now, nothing seemed the same. He told one of his men that he "never thought any place could be so changed."

Drake still vowed to strike it rich before returning home. But he never saw England again. Like John Hawkins before him, Drake suddenly fell sick. His condition quickly worsened. At 4 A.M. on January 27, 1596, he summoned a few members of his crew. He wanted them to help him put on his armor so that he "might die like a soldier." An hour later, the old pirate took his last breath.

Drake's body was put in a lead coffin. Musicians played trumpets. The whole fleet fired cannons. Then the men pushed his coffin overboard. The sea was where Drake had spent the best years of his life. The sea was where he made his fortune and fame. And now the sea was where the amazing story of Francis Drake came to an end.

GUNS FIRE as Sir Francis Drake's coffin is dropped into the sea. The old seaman would be remembered as England's greatest navigator, a war hero, a slave trader, a deserter, a murderous pirate, and the terror of Spain.

Wicked?

During his last, doomed voyage to the New World, Sir Francis Drake sat down to write a letter. He addressed it to the Spanish governor of Puerto Rico. Drake's attack on the island had just failed, and at least 25 of his men were now Spanish prisoners. Drake wanted to make sure they were treated well.

Drake wrote that he had always treated his Spanish prisoners "honorably and mercifully, and I have set many of them free." And as strange as it may sound, this was more or less true. Francis Drake was a pirate and a thief. But he rarely killed or tortured his prisoners. In fact, he often showered captured Spanish officers with gifts. He even invited them to eat with him.

During his long and bloody career, Drake was full of contradictions. In his twenties, he took part in slave-trading expeditions. Later, he fought side-by-side with escaped Africans against the Spanish. At one point,

Drake discovered that a Spanish soldier had murdered an African child. Drake became so angry that he executed two captured Spanish friars in revenge.

Like many people of his time, Drake was driven by religious hatred. In the 16th century, Protestants and Catholics both firmly believed that they had God on their side. They saw their enemies not as mere human beings but as agents of the devil. Spanish soldiers who caught Protestant intruders in the New World often slaughtered them by the hundreds.

But Drake's main motivation was not religion. Nor was it patriotism. It was greed. He could display immense courage when he saw a chance to make money. But he saw no reason to risk his life and his ships when there was no hope of personal gain. To some people, that made him a coward. To Francis Drake, it was the attitude that made him the greatest pirate of his time.

Timeline of Terror

1540

c. 1540: Francis Drake is born.

1559: Queen Elizabeth I outlaws Catholic worship, making England a Protestant country.

1562: John Hawkins launches the English slave trade with kidnapping raids on the African coast.

1567–68: Drake captains a ship on a slave raid and eventually deserts Hawkins in the Caribbean.

1569: Drake marries Mary Newman.

1571: Drake commands his first raiding expedition to the Caribbean.

1573: With help from Africans and the French, Drake steals a fortune in gold and silver from the Spanish in Panama.

1577–80: Drake sails around the world, raiding the Spanish in South America along the way.

1581: Queen Elizabeth I knights Drake.

1586: Drake attacks Santo Domingo during a failed raid in the Caribbean.

1586: Starving English colonists in Roanoke are rescued by Drake's ships.

1587: Drake launches a successful attack on the Spanish and Portuguese coasts, delaying the Armada's invasion by one year.

1588: Drake serves as a vice admiral during the English defeat of the Spanish Armada.

1596: Drake dies in the Caribbean after a failed attempt to seize Panama from the Spanish.

1596

Glossary

adept (uh-DEPT) *adjective* able to do something very well

alliance (uh-LYE-uhnss) *noun* an agreement to work together

armada (ar-MAH-duh) *noun* a large group of warships

arrant (AIR-uhnt) *adjective* completely, totally

artillery (ar-TIL-uh-ree) *noun* large, powerful guns

audacious (aw-DAY-shus) *adjective* showing a willingness to take bold risks

beacon (BEE-kuhn) *noun* a light or fire used as a signal or for guidance

captive (KAP-tiv) *noun* a person who has been captured

colony (KOL-uh-nee) *noun* a territory that has been settled by people from another country and is controlled by that country

desertion (di-ZUR-shun) *noun* the act of running away from a person or duty without permission

devastated (DEV-uh-stay-tid) *adjective* experiencing great distress

diabolical (dye-uh-BOL-i-kuhl) *adjective* extremely wicked

disillusioned (diss-i-LOO-zhuhnd) *adjective* disappointed that something or someone is not as good as one had believed

ducat (DUK-et) *noun* a gold coin formerly used as money in many European countries

exploit (ek-SPLOIT) *noun* a heroic or famous deed

fortification (FOR-tuh-fi-cay-shun) *noun* walls and other works built to defend a place from attack

implicate (IM-pluh-kayt) *verb* to indicate that someone is or has been involved in a misdeed

interrogation (in-ter-uh-GAY-shun) *noun* a formal and detailed questioning session knight (NITE) *noun* in England, a man who has been given the title "Sir" as a reward for service to his country

mariner (MA-rih-nur) *noun* a sailor

marauder (muh-RAW-duhr) *noun* someone who raids and plunders

mentor (MEN-tor) *noun* an experienced and trusted adviser or teacher

merchant ship (MUR-chuhnt SHIP) *noun* a ship that carries goods for trade

monastery (MON-uh-ster-ee) *noun* a group of buildings where monks live and work

mutiny (MYOOT-uh-nee) *noun* a revolt against someone in charge, especially while at sea

nobility (noh-BIL-ih-tee) *noun* the people in a country or state who have been born into wealthy families and have the highest social rank

pardon (PARD-uhn) *noun* the forgiving of a crime by the government

pessimistic (pess-uh-MISS-tik) *adjective* thinking that the worst will happen

plunder (PLUHN-dur) *verb* to steal things by force

Protestant (PROT-uh-stuhnt) *noun* a Christian who does not belong to the Roman Catholic Church or Orthodox Church

relentless (ri-LENT-liss) *adjective* extremely determined and unwilling to give up

secluded (si-KLOO-did) *adjective* sheltered and private

strait (STRAYT) *noun* a narrow strip of water that connects two larger bodies of water

transatlantic (tran-zuht-LAN-tik) *adjective* crossing the Atlantic Ocean

venture (VEN-chur) *noun* a project that is somewhat risky

vulnerability (vuhl-nur-uh-BIL-i-tee) *noun* a weakness that exposes someone or something to attack

FIND OUT MORE

Here are some books and websites with more information about Sir Francis Drake and his times.

BOOKS

Donkin, Andrew. Sir Francis Drake and His Daring Deeds (Horribly Famous). London: Scholastic, 2006. (176 pages) *Illustrated with black and white cartoons, this account of Sir Francis Drake's life is both factual and entertaining.*

Eding, June. Who Was Queen Elizabeth? New York: Grosset & Dunlap, 2008. (112 pages) *A biography of the famous queen who sent Francis Drake on many expeditions and military missions.*

Gallagher, Jim. Sir Francis Drake and the Foundation of a World Empire. Philadelphia: Chelsea House, 2001. (63 pages) *An appealing, well-written account of the life of Sir Francis Drake and his impact on the world.*

Rice, Earle. Sir Francis Drake: Navigator and Pirate (Great Explorations). New York: Benchmark Books, 2003. (76 pages) *A thorough account of the extraordinary life of Sir Francis Drake.*

Stewart, David. You Wouldn't Want to Explore with Sir Francis Drake! New York: Franklin Watts, 2005. (32 pages) *Illustrated with humorous cartoons, this book explores the unpleasant side of sailing with Sir Francis Drake.*

WEBSITES

http://www.fordham.edu/halsall/mod/1580pretty-drake.html
A first person account of Drake's around-the-world voyage, written by one his sailors

http://www.goldenhinde.org
The visitor-information site for the Golden Hinde, *a replica of the ship that Drake sailed around the world.*

http://www.loc.gov/rr/rarebook/catalog/drake/drake-home.html
Sir Francis Drake: A Pictorial Biography, *by Hans P. Kraus, is a digitized book from the Library of Congress. It includes some fascinating primary-source illustrations and materials.*

http://www.mariner.org/educationalad/ageofex/drake.php
A brief biography of Francis Drake from the website of the Mariners' Museum of Newport News, Virginia.

For Grolier subscribers:
http://go.grolier.com/ searches: Drake, Sir Francis; Elizabeth I, Queen of England; Spanish Armada; pirate; Atlantic slave trade

Author's Note and Bibliography

Perhaps the most famous story about Francis Drake describes his composure on the day the Spanish Armada appeared off the coast of England. Supposedly, Drake was playing lawn bowling when the news reached Plymouth. The other English sea captains began to dash off to their ships, but Drake remained cool. "We still have time to finish the game and to thrash the Spaniards, too," he calmly declared.

Writers, painters, and filmmakers have told this story again and again.

There's only one problem. The story probably isn't true. It was first told many years after Drake died.

Writing about Drake is challenging in part because his story is so full of myths. One tale even has him defeating the Armada by magic.

It would be nice to know how Drake viewed his own adventures, but he never bothered to write his story down. I've tried to make those adventures come alive while leaving out the myths. Was Drake good, wicked, or something in between?

The following sources have been the most useful in writing this book:

Andrews, Kenneth R. **Drake's Voyages: A Re-assessment of Their Place in Elizabethan Maritime Expansion.** London: Weidenfeld and Nicolson, 1967.

Cummins, John. **Francis Drake: The Lives of a Hero.** New York: St. Martin's Press, 1995.

Keeler, Mary Frear, ed. **Sir Francis Drake's West Indian Voyage, 1585–86.** London: Hakluyt Society, 1981.

Kelsey, Harry. **Sir Francis Drake: The Queen's Pirate.** New Haven and London: Yale University Press, 1998.

Sugden, John. **Sir Francis Drake.** New York: Henry Holt, 1990.

Whitfield, Peter, **Sir Francis Drake.** New York: New York University Press, 2004.

Wright, Irene A., trans. and ed. **Further English Voyages to Spanish America, 1583–1594: Documents from the Archives of the Indies at Seville Illustrating English Voyages to the Caribbean, the Spanish Main, Florida, and Virginia.** London: The Hakluyt Society, 1951.

—Charles Nick